THE LOTUS' LOVE SUITE

The Lotus' Love Suite
Ashley A.T.

The Lotus' Love Suite

Copyright © 2017 Ashley Spencer

ISBN: 978-0-692-89997-7

Kingdom Scribes Publishing, LLC.
www.kingdom-scribes.com

Graphics by DT Web Designs

All rights reserved. No part of this book may be used or reproduced in any manner whatsoever without written permission, except in the case of brief quotations embodied in critical articles or reviews.

DEDICATED TO

Love, Heartbreak, & Healing

Because you made me feel things I didn't know it was possible to feel. And I took the joy and the pain, and decided to let it all out here.

Thank you. -A

CONTENTS

INTRODUCTION... 10
STAGE I
    INFINITY... 13
    GOALS.. 15
    KING.. 16
    CLUES.. 18
    PROMISES... 19
STAGE II
    BLIND LOVE...................................... 24
    A LIGHT FOR THE DARK.................. 27
    SECURITY... 29
    OF ALL THE PLACES...................... 31
    EUPHORIA.. 33
    THE MOTIONS OF DEVOTION........ 35
    GRATITUDE..................................... 37
STAGE III
    BABYGIRL.. 44
    DESERTS.. 45
    PAIN... 47
    MORPHINE...................................... 49
    THE ART OF LETTING GO.............. 51
STAGE IV
    GHOSTS.. 57
    MIRROR... 59
    WHAT IF... 61
    NEW BEGINNINGS.......................... 63
    THE LOTUS FLOWER   65

It was so much more than either of us could have ever imagined…

Introduction to the Love Suite

Close your eyes and take a walk with me
Open your mind, use your heart to see
Let go and relax, like a petal drifting down a stream
I'd like to introduce you to the Lotus' Love Suite.
Here, my heart's desires manifest and come to life
Here, Love has a home, and even when it's wrong, it's still right
Happiness levels reach heights unparalleled
But below awaits my own personal hell.
My darkest fears may follow, but only for the night
The Lotus must push through the dark mud
For its beauty to be seen by the light.

STAGE I: Potential

Infinity

A little girl once dreamed that one day a man named Love would come and sweep her off her feet
Through hell and heartbreak here I am still dreaming of the same thing;
Still searching for Infinity.

In a love that lasts for all of eternity
Worth so much more than any amount of money
Enough to buy a lifetime of happiness and peace
And satisfy a woman with a little girl's dream.

The Most High's gift of life is comprised of three things;
Faith, Hope, and Love. And Love is the greatest of these.
When all else should fail, true Love remains never ending
So if I look for Love, I'll surely find Infinity.
And once I've found him, together we'll plant a field of Love's seeds
And raise children who hold the potential for infinite possibilities
And carry generations of a dream across undiscovered galaxies and into unthought of centuries.

Basically,
Until the day that space and time should meet
Until Love is found and my journey is complete
Until I've manifested a little girl's dreams
From this day on, I'll be searching for Infinity.

*What's the difference between Dreams and Reality?
   The same thing that pushes a flower, out of a tiny seed.*

Goals

There is a love within me
A love that resonates so deep
Resounding in every cell of my body
Longing to be shared with somebody.
To love another is everything I could need
Everything to make my dreams a reality.
A love that grants me someone to hold
To be there with me until love is all I know
To speak of love until no love's been untold
And until love is all that remains of two souls.

Love is the goal.

King

I've had visions of what the two of us could be
I caught a glimpse of our dynasty in my wildest dreams
I felt his tender touch caress me in my sleep
And awoke absolutely sure that when found his soul I'd keep

Have you seen my King?
His skin glistens like chocolate coated honey
Begging for me to indulge in all his melanated glory
I long for the brother humbly walking the streets
Unaware that he's the very King I seek

I thought I found you in him,
But he only wanted the benefits of being a friend.
I thought I saw you in another him,
He caught my eye, but lacked substance within.
So my search continues, seemingly without an end.

But I know you're out there, I feel it
Hidden clearly in plain sight.
If my heart is my guide, one day my King
Will finally be brought to the light.

*And suddenly I caught sight of you,
And the Lotus seed sprouted a root.*

Clues

Time creates the path, that leads to the clues,
Each one I find reveals more about you.
The more that I discover, the more that I'm drawn to
As I try so desperately to solve the mystery of you.

Waiting to see what may befall,
But so far I can say that I'm captivated by you, flaws and all.
Time spent with you leaves me simply in awe,
Leaving me longing for more, until I've seen it all.

Time creates the path that leads to the clues,
I'm hoping to find the ones that reveal more of you.
Anxious to discover, eager to find the truth,
Ready to solve the mystery of you.

Promise

You want love.
I can feel it.
I see it in your eyes,
You can't conceal it.
Longing to express love,
but you're afraid to admit it.
Afraid that you'll get hurt,
trust me I know.
I've been there before,
through Love's highs and lows.

Afraid you'll give too much
If you let your heart show.
But what you give I'll return,
So our two halves can build one whole.

Let go of your doubts, put
your trust in me. There's
no need to worry, I'll be
everything you need. From
the air in my lungs
to the blood that I bleed,
The love inside of me
is all yours to keep.

Any time, any day
If you want me I'm right here.
All I ask is for your love,

I just need you dear.
In December or next May
If you need me I'll be near.
All I ask is that you trust me,
With my love, you have nothing to fear.

STAGE II: Growth

*With the foundation laid and the roots in place,
I couldn't wait to find the Love we could create*

Blind Love

Can I love you with my eyes closed?
I heard it takes a blind heart to fall in love with the soul.
Cause somehow seeing less always reveals so much more
So blindly I find the intent of your heart as I explore

I find that when we embrace, though my eyes see separate beings,
In the darkness, we become one whole
So when you're away, in the light of the day, I close my eyes and you're never far from home

And when you return
And sweet words from your lips fall breathlessly like soft kisses onto my collarbone
They carry in them hand-written love letters from the depths of a lover's heart and soul
With my eyes closed I feel your flow and it feels like the love I've been dying to know
That and much more you and I could find if we close our eyes
As we fall in love with each other's soul

Why do opposites attract
Like the Earth and the Sky?
For the same reason that a flower grows from the dark soil
Because of the love from the Light

A Light for the Dark

Dark
Like deep blue ocean,
Yet a shallow surface
is what I found
I reached in deep
For the heart in your sea
But my fingers only touched
a shallow ground;
Your dark waters were empty
But I found a way to see.

With light that reaches
To beyond infinity
Illuminated by my
God given divinity
With enough brightness
For both you and me
To find the depth of your oceans
For the rest of eternity;
My heart is yours,
Until the very end of time.

The heavens and earth Will
know a brighter sky
The sea will find depth
From the love of you and I
There'll never be a day
Where you'll have to cry

And I'll share the same fate
As long as our love never dies.
Though the ocean dark
With the light,
We found the depths of life

Security

He held my face in his hands,
Gazed down at me with such intensity
It made me all but forget how to breathe.
His thumb so softly stroked my cheek
As if his fingerprint declared,
"You precious thing, you belong to me."

If unrequited love was ever in my worry
He reassured my loyalty with abundant reciprocity
Finding ways to show, no empty words would he ever speak
His demonstrations would tell me
That I'm all he could ever love, want, and need.

His hands are my safe haven,
There's no other place I'd rather be
He's locked me up in his love,
And allowed my soul to be set free
Wrapped up in his arms,
And protected by his love for me
He's all that I could ever need.
I've found in him complete security.

Of All the Places

Of all the places that a tree could be
How did this one end up here, so perfectly?
By chance it grew from a tiny seed
And became a home where a blue bird sleeps.

Out of all the fish found in the sea
The red snapper by far is the best one to eat.
Battered and fried in the right mix of flour and seasoning
Something that tastes this good was surely meant to be

Of all the stars we can and can't see
Why was the sun chosen to light up this galaxy?
Did it find its place by gravity or destiny?
Either way the Earth is lucky to be blessed by its light and heat.

So how rare is it that when fate and time should meet
That I found you so casually lying here next to me
When God planned this moment, it wasn't coincidence where we'd be
Like a phenomenon of the galaxy, He made it your destiny
To be the reason why I'm happy.

Of all the places…

Any stem with leaves can sprout from a seed, but I think a soil filled with love is what gives a flower its intoxicating beauty

Euphoria

It's this euphoric state of mind
That you got me in, all the time.

Blissfully ascending into the skies,
Like being drawn into Heaven
Through golden rays of sunshine.
Drifting away on Cloud 99,
As your love caresses me
With soft kisses down my spine.

Amongst the clouds, there is an infinite symphony
That plays all night just for you and me.
The drums are banging
To the tempo of our hearts' beat,
As the instruments play
With the passion that flows through the sheets
And the love that we've made to its sweet music
Has indisputably inspired all the muses
They're gratified as they consume it
The way they love our sweet Love's music.

From the skies, they dispel on us appeased sighs
That inflate us with such elated highs
Like from the feeling I get
When I look in your eyes
Or like this euphoric state of mind
That you got me in. All. The. Time.

The Motions of Devotion

It was so much more than either of us could have imagined. Like a halo-dawning dream you wouldn't believe could be fathomed. The slightest touch between us created so much more than just lust. The look in your eyes was something more like a deep love. Guided by pure intuition, we slowly walked into a sea of amorous disposition. You found me; Delicate yet enticing. And then I found you; Tenderly caressing my body.

Our deepest desires met in a passion fueled fire, and our love was responsible for the actions that transpired. Our souls, overwhelming with emotions, cried out for rigorous devotions of fluid motions, shared between two lovers caught up in a web of each other, where every stroke only drew us closer. Closer to our climax, the peak of the mountain where love resides at, where we balance because every time I push you away, you always pull me right back, never leaving me, yet still pushing me further.

Further until I can't take it, until I swear I can't make it, and then you look me in the eyes and tell me to "Embrace it." So I let go and let your soul inside and touches me in places I didn't know you could find. Then it meets mine and our two souls collide. And we're swept away to a cloud in the sky and then heavens rejoice and we see God smile. And in that moment, let it be known that all was right. If only for that moment, I was yours and you were mine. And together we made love, all through the night, and made devotions to love for the rest of our lives.

Gratitude

It's crazy how he makes me feel …
Conditioned to think that Love would kill
I used to think that a love like this was unreal
But now I love how my love's love feels

I sing song for the feelings I can't say
My cheeks stay flushed, thinking about the love we make
He's on my mind all day
He brings to my life the things for which I've prayed

With eyes that send chills down my spine
And lips that know what's on my mind
Words that flow like a stream of wine
That speak of a love so gentle, of a love so kind.

He builds me up, and it makes me weak.
I fear for what his love will mean to me.
Of how this will go, I can't foresee
But I can't help but thank God for my love,
And his name is…

Tragedy

*Because nothing is ever as it really seems…
And while the Lotus reaches for the light
It may never see the storm clouds lurking.*

Stage III: Tragedy

*The first cloud that came was Insecurity.
The second was Lack of Trust... and poured out a Lack of
Loyalty*

*And then the thunder roared with Threats
And when the lightning struck, you moved onto the Next
And I was left, singed with Regrets.*

Babygirl

You called me Babygirl, and it sounded so perfect
It made me feel like everything I'd been through was finally worth it.
All that wishing and waiting, all those long nights I spent praying,
For God to find the right one for me, and for Love to finally let me be happy.
And I'm forever grateful, for God to have let it all come true,
Forever indebted to the Fates, who sent me someone like you…

So forgive me if I'm having a hard time…
It's just kind of hard to accept that you're no longer mine.
It's kind of hard to know, I'll search for but never find,
Another love like yours to fill this empty heart of mine.
And yeah, I go by a new name, my new lover calls me bae
But for some reason it just doesn't sound right,
His love just doesn't feel the same.

Deserts

So this is it . . . This is what I'm left with?
We travelled through the jungle and I ended up in the desert because I took a wrong exit?
The signs all said "Come, you'll be free!" and "Don't look at this glass as half empty!"
But said nothing about roaming a sand-filled sea
And what good is being free when a cactus is your only company?

The jungle may be so dense that you can only catch a glimpse of the light. And dangerous creatures are on the prowl morning, noon, and night
But I was always safe with you by my side . . .
So now I'm sitting in the desert trying to figure out why
One fight made me go left, when you were still standing to my right.

How is the desert filled to the brim with so much emptiness?
Why is the only shadow I can find cast from a cactus?
I love sunshine, but I'd really love some shade from the heat.
And I'm a tree lover, but I can only get so close to the cactus before it hurts me.

In the mornings, I sit next to the cactus in its shade
But by noon, the sun is high its shadow fades away
So I roam the sand-filled seas, until the end of the day.
But without you by my side, I'm alone in the cold desert night
So I dream of the jungle, your warm embrace, and even long

for another fight.

Pain

Lord help me please, I can't take it, I'm begging for mercy
It's driving me crazy, check me in, I plead insanity
Can't you see how bad I'm hurting and in need of relief?
It's just not right for me to feel these things.
Sleep don't bring peace cause it haunts me in my dreams
Antagonizing me, thrashing around in the deepest parts of me
Until I wake up in cold sweats and the sound of my screams
The tears on my cheeks flow from my soul that's crying
My heart is black and blue from fighting the feelings I keep denying
You said you loved me, and it hurts so bad to know that you were lying.
The only thing that hurts more?
Is seeing you and her . . .
Together . . .
And smiling.

Morphine

I misdiagnosed.
I prescribed myself the right version of the wrong dose.
Reminiscing as if remembering could erase memories,
Addicted to the drug like addiction was the remedy.
Morphine hides the pain from the heart you broke
Memories take me away, now I'm addicted to both.

Flashbacks and relapse leave me overstimulated
I take flashbacks and get relapsed until I'm completely sedated.
What I thought would bring some kind of healing
Now leave me all but numb to its feeling
Your love was like morphine and Lord knows I still crave it.
The memories feel good but can never be recreated.

As the syringe breaks the skin pain becomes pure bliss
The needle eases in as I slowly inject the memory of your kiss.
The furthest from the real thing...
But the closest substance to a remedy...
There aren't many things that feel quite like this
And this Morphine comes second to all the thing about you
that I miss.

The Art of Letting Go

I see the desperation written all over her face
As she takes, yet another, Deep. Long. Sigh.
She holds on, maybe just a little too tight
To the sweet relief
She finds in each breath's release.
Yet exasperation and pain
So faithfully remain
The source of her undying need to seek alleviation
The vital salvation
Now found in trivial things,
Like the way she breathes.
The endless despair consumes her in every way
Day in. Day out. Till it drives her insane.
It takes all she has
To find a reason to stay alive
Fighting to have the faith
To know that the pain will subside
Yet there's nothing left she can do or say
She's tried everything
And the pain still remains
The wave of despair washes her up
Leaves her out to dry
She lies on the ground
As the tears fill her eyes
And she holds on maybe just a little too tight
To the desperation that gives her the strength for one last try
Praying this time that the pain will subside
As she takes, yet another, Deep. Long. Sigh.

As unbearable as pain might be, isn't it crazy that pain won't kill you? As unbearable as pain might be, isn't it crazy that your hurt can heal you?

*As harsh as the rain can be,
a flower still needs water to grow.
As harsh as the rain can be,
the storm will pass and the Lotus' beauty will show.*

Stage IV: Recovery

Ghosts

Sometimes acceptance hurts more than grief
It's like letting go of the ghosts you still see
Or giving up on everything you once believed
Or remembering how I felt a part of me die
The day I realized our story was complete.

And how it crushed my heart
to hear those things you said to me
And how I hoped and prayed that those were bitter lies
and words filled with deceit
Cause accepting all of that means I have to be strong
when I still feel so weak
But the cold hard truth finally came to me
Looked me in the face and said "You've got to move on,
He's gone, you watched him leave."
Then left me alone in my tears and memories.

I cried until I was all cried out,
Until the tears washed away my grief.
And found that ghosts of my memories
Were filled with the message that would save me.

*"Since hurting people are the ones who hurt others,
Maybe if we can learn to love ourselves,
With flowers bruised and battered by Life's weather,
Then we can also learn to love each other."*

Mirror

And then I opened my eyes to see a little clearer
Then I saw her there, my inner child, staring at me through the mirror
And she studied the pain written all over my face
Until we found the words I'd been trying to hear her say

You've been through heartbreaks before
And trust me you'll go through many more
There'll be better days and there'll be some much worse
But trust me girl you've got the strength to endure.

And I smiled and reached out to give her a hug
But I only felt the glass when our hands touched
And she said "Go. Turn around so you can show the world some love
And give them all what you would have gave to us
From you to them to him to her to them then back to you until the cycle is done
And then, maybe then, the world will finally know love.

What If...?

What if God condemned us for the first sin that we made,
Would the number of angels in heaven still be the same?
Would He send us to hell, pay no attention to our cries of pain?
And decide to ignore us when we ask for forgiveness when we prayed?

Or would he show us mercy, give us a chance at salvation once again?
Let us learn from our lessons and make use of the wisdom we've gained.

What if our parents abandoned us when we misbehaved?
Could we have survived without them, would these children even last a day?
Would mom and dad turn us over to the world only to become its prey,
If they felt like we didn't deserve them every time we disobeyed?
Or would they have the patience to raise their seeds and show us the right way?
Take us back in their arms and watch us grow as we play.

What if the ones we loved were too quick to turn to hate?
Would they damn your loyalty and throw it all away?
Could you fight to show them of what you're really made,
When they choose to overlook the good times because of one mistake?
Or would they remember the times when they fell short and

show you empathy?
Finding the patience of a parent or His everlasting mercy.

New Beginnings

As sure as the Sun rises
with the new day,
The things promised tomorrow
will come if we have faith.
If it is in His will, I'll
patiently wait. For if
there is a will,
there surely is a way.

Not knowing how,
unsure of when,
But certain that all things
follow a trend.
As it was in the beginning,
It shall be in the end.
So I have no doubt,
that one day Love
Will find me again.

The Lotus Flower

As beautiful as she is now
was not always this way.
Her journey began trapped in a bud
submerged in an endless abyss.
A never-ending darkness of night,
Hidden away from the day,
Never knowing of the light.

In the murky waters that surround her,
Hopelessness and Loneliness
are her only friends.
Quick to wrap her fresh leaves with their lies
of a life of pain that never ends.
Reminding her that it's found in every direction.
Reminding her that it never ends.

Yet the budding Lotus refuses to accept
that things are this way
Even if the night is all she knows.
Something in her dreams of the Sun's golden rays
But rumors of a Day are hard to believe
When there's no proof of it to show
in the dark night's endless sea.
Yet she knows there's something more
Even as a small bud she feels it in her core.

Let's call it faith
The strength to believe in a love we've yet to see.

Drawing her to the light lying just beyond the surface of the sea
A beautiful Lotus emerges from the dark waters
Finally, the sunshine is all she sees.
How refreshing for her to know
that these things exist outside of dreams

Though the leaves that once protected her as a bud are stained,
And on them the darkness of her past visibly remains,
the Lotus flower's red petals filled with passion
tell a different story
Untouched by her days of pain
Colored by an enduring hope for love
Called faith.

I am the Lotus.
I've finally seen the Sun's golden rays

ABOUT THE AUTHOR

Ashley A.T. is a writer based out of Atlanta, GA. Born and raised just outside of Miami, FL. Ashley was the oldest of two girls born to her parents. Her father, a now retired officer of the military, and her mother, an experienced educator, both encouraged and helped their girls to achieve academic success and develop their personal talents. As a child, Ashley was always highly creative and took rigorous classes that allowed her to read and learn to write extensively about a variety of subjects. As she grew up, becoming a hopeless romantic, she used writing to express the emotions she would feel while falling in and out of love. In college, she discovered a new outlet for her writing abilities after joining the journalism club and writing for the college newspaper.

As Ashley continued her education; information technology courses and additional electives, with a focus on the arts, strategically stimulated her passion for writing through assignments where she wrote essays, articles, analyses about different subjects and through various creative expressions. Through her love of music, Ashley began to take interest in the poetic nature of songwriting, and started writing poetry her senior year of college, and has since acquired an online following after sharing her poems about love and life. After graduating and moving to Atlanta for an IT job, Ashley AT is now breaking into the urban writing scene through her blog, social media platforms, and poetry, to inspire a new generation of readers, by writing from the heart with a mission to spread a message about the power of Love, Peace and Light.

Ashley A.T.
@_OfTheAshTree

Contact the Author
www.ashley-at.com

Contact the Publisher
www.kingdom-scribes.com
Now Accepting Manuscripts

www.ingramcontent.com/pod-product-compliance
Lightning Source LLC
Chambersburg PA
CBHW031429290426
44110CB00011B/585